DESTINY

Choosing to Change
the Course of Your Life

CHARLES R.
SWINDOLL

INSIGHT FOR LIVING

DESTINY
Choosing to Change the Course of Your Life

From the Bible-Teaching Ministry of Charles R. Swindoll

Charles R. Swindoll has devoted his life to the clear, practical teaching and application of God's Word and His grace. Chuck currently is the senior pastor of Stonebriar Community Church in Frisco, Texas; but his listening audience extends far beyond this local church body. As a leading program in Christian broadcasting, *Insight for Living* airs in major Christian radio markets around the world, reaching people groups in languages they can understand. Chuck's extensive writing ministry has also served the body of Christ worldwide and his leadership as president and now chancellor of Dallas Theological Seminary has helped prepare and equip a new generation for ministry.

Published by IFL Publishing House, A Division of Insight for Living
Post Office Box 251007, Plano, Texas 75025-1007

Editor in Chief: Cynthia Swindoll, President, Insight for Living
Vice President: Wayne Stiles, Th.M., D.Min., Dallas Theological Seminary
Editors: Mark Gaither, Th.M., Dallas Theological Seminary
        Brie Engeler, B.A., University Scholars, Baylor University
Proofreaders: Mike Penn, B.A., Journalism, University of Oklahoma
        Melissa Carlisle, M.A., Christian Education,
        Dallas Theological Seminary
Cover Designer: Kari Pratt, B.A., Commercial Art, Southwestern
        Oklahoma State University
Production Artist: Nancy Gallaher, B.F.A., Advertising Art,
        University of North Texas
Back Cover Photo: David Edmonson, Photographer

ISBN 1-57972-694-1

DESTINY

**Choosing to Change
the Course of Your Life**

INTRODUCTION

Most of us don't like to contemplate subjects like death—or life after death—until circumstances grab us by the collar and force us to stare the questions in the face.

We lose a spouse, a parent, a child, a friend . . . and suddenly life-and-death issues no longer seem vague and distant. They become very real and must somehow be addressed.

Even more shocking is when the death we contemplate is our own. The doctor calls us back into the office and presents us with facts we don't want to hear and don't know how to handle. A life that seemed somehow interminable— indestructible—is reduced to a matter of months . . . perhaps weeks.

In an instant, issues like "eternal destiny" snap into sharp focus. Suddenly, questions about our soul and salvation seem acutely relevant. Questions we once hesitated to ponder or voice now scream to be answered . . .

- "How can I know God in a meaningful way?"

- "What must I do to guarantee eternal life with my Maker?"

- "Is there some way I can be certain that I will go to heaven?"

- "Will you explain in simple, nontechnical terms what it means to be born again?"

- "I'm guilty because I haven't lived a clean life. How can the Lord forgive me?"

- "I've been a fairly religious person, but I lack a deep and abiding peace with God . . . why?"

- "What does the Bible say about life after death?"

- "Did Jesus actually die for me?"

- "What, exactly, is the gospel?"

Whether or not these questions are verbalized, they are the ones most people think about, especially when death seems near. They are good questions that deserve an answer. They are also searching questions that have to do with an issue of utmost importance—being forgiven and entering into eternal life from God. This is not something that calls for a lot of opinions. Theological double-talk will do nothing to settle our disquieted souls. The insights must come from the Bible. They need to be so clear that anybody can understand them. They also have to make sense.

Here is a scriptural, simple, sensible answer for those who wonder about the single most significant subject in all of life: salvation.

Chuck Swindoll

Charles R. Swindoll

SINCERELY LOST

Being lost is a terrifying experience. A person's head spins as panic creeps up, shouting threats like, "You'll never find your way!" or "It's impossible!" Fear clutches at you.

When I was about eight years old, I remember being lost downtown in the busy metropolis of Houston, Texas. My mother had told me to stay in the toy department of a store while she went down the street to pick up a package she was having gift-wrapped. I continued to play for a few minutes but soon lost interest. So I decided to leave the store and walk down to where my mom had gone. Bad decision. I turned the wrong way, so I was going in the opposite direction, all the time being absolutely sure it was the right way.

I must have walked four long blocks before I realized my mistake. I thought, "Maybe it's across the street." My heart began beating faster as I trotted over to the other side, but I still couldn't find the store. By then I had run five, maybe six blocks . . . still no sign of that familiar store-front.

I began to cry. I didn't know who to ask for help . . . everybody seemed so unconcerned. My mind was seized with such fear that I couldn't even remember the name of the store where she said she was going or even the store I had left twenty minutes before. I circled back toward the direction I began — or so I thought — but in my bewildered state, I had made yet another miscalculation, for nothing looked at all familiar now.

To this day, I distinctly recall the awful sense of desperation and confusion. Guilt assaulted me as I said to myself again and again. *Why didn't I do as Mama told me? Why didn't I obey?*

The strange part of it all was that there were people all around me — hundreds of them — and within a few feet there were cars filling the street, moving in both directions. There was also a policeman at each intersection, as well as numerous employees and merchants inside every store I passed. There I was, darting here and there surrounded by all that humanity, but I was completely lost. I could not have felt more lost in the thick jungles along the Amazon!

Through the kindness of a total stranger who saw my plight and took the time to talk to me and to escort me back to the original toy department, I was rescued and reunited with my concerned, loving mother. Although I am more than sixty years removed from that horrible episode, I vividly remember how terrifying it was. Being lost is awful.

Several strange things are true about being lost. One is that we can think we really aren't when we are. Sincerity is no guarantee we're on the right road. Furthermore, we don't have to be alone to be lost. We can be surrounded by a lot of folks—even a large group of nice people—and be totally off track. Running faster doesn't help, either. Speed, like sincerity, is no friend to the bewildered.

One more thought: We can't trust our feelings or our hunches to solve our dilemma. We need help from something or someone outside ourselves. A map. A person who knows the way. Whatever or whoever . . . we must have accurate assistance.

Hurtling toward a Destiny . . . Unaware

It's interesting to note that one of the terms the Bible uses to describe people who don't know God in a personal and meaningful manner is "lost." That doesn't necessarily mean they are immoral or lawless or bad neighbors or financial failures or emotionally unstable or unfriendly folks. Just lost. As we've already observed, they may be sincere, involved, in touch with many people, and moving rapidly (and successfully) through life. They may even feel good about themselves — confident, secure, enthusiastic . . . yet still lost. Physically active and healthy yet spiritually off track. Sincerely deluded. Unconsciously moving through life and out of touch with the One who made them. Disconnected and distant from the living God.

Take a close look at this statement I've copied from the old, reliable book of Proverbs in the Bible.

> There is a way which seems right to a
> man, but its end is the way of death.
> (Proverbs 14:12)

Isn't that penetrating? The "way" a person is going through life may seem right. It may have the appearance of being okay. It may also have the approval and admiration of other rather influential individuals. But its end result is the ultimate dead-end street.

All this reminds me of a tragic, yet true, World War II story. The *Lady-Be-Good* was a bomber whose crew was a well-seasoned flight team, a group of intelligent and combat-ready airmen. After a successful bombing mission, they were returning to home base late one night.

In front of the pilot was a panel of instruments and radar equipment they had to rely on to reach their final destination. They had made the flight many times before, so they knew about how long it took to return.

But this flight was different. Apparently unaware of a strong tailwind that pushed the bomber much more rapidly through the night air than usual, the men in the cockpit looked in amazement at their instruments as they signaled that it was time to descend and land. That didn't seem right.

As a result, they refused to believe those accurate dials and gauges. Confident that they were still many miles from home, they kept flying and hoping, looking intently for familiar lights below. The fuel supply was finally depleted. The bomber never made it back. Sixteen years later, it was found deep in the desert. Its fine crew had all perished, having overshot the field by a great distance . . . because they followed the promptings of their own feelings, which "seemed right" but proved to be wrong. Dead wrong.

What happened in the air back in the early 1940s is happening in principle every day on earth. There are good, sincere, well-meaning, intelligent people traveling on a collision course with death yet totally unaware of their destiny.

That's why we read that Jesus, God's great Son, came "to seek and to save that which was lost" (Luke 19:10). His coming to earth was God's seek-and-save mission designed to help those who are lost find the right way home.

That needs some explanation.

Think of the Bible as the absolutely reliable instrument panel designed to get people (and to keep people) on the right track. We won't be confused if we believe its signals and respond to its directions, even though we may not "feel" in agreement at times. In this Book we find a bold yet true statement:

> God has given us eternal life, and this life is in His Son. He who has the Son has the life; he who does not have the Son of God does not have the life. These things I have written to you who believe in the name of the Son of God, so that you may know that you have eternal life. (1 John 5:11–13)

Read that again, this time a little more slowly and, if possible, aloud.

Salvation Offered — Free

It doesn't take a Ph.D. in English Literature to observe that God is offering a gift. The gift is eternal life, which is directly connected to His Son. Now let's be clear and cautious. Becoming a member of a church is not mentioned here — just believing in the Son of God, Jesus Christ. Neither does God require a long list of heavy-duty accomplishments. Nor vast sums of money. God is coming to the rescue of those who are lost by offering the free gift of eternal life to those who will simply believe. Those who do believe will know they have been rescued (Romans 8:16).

No mumbo-jumbo, no tricks, no divinely hidden agenda, no cleverly concealed conditions. The lost can be certain they are on the right road by trusting what God is signaling from His panel of truth. Believe Him!

"But it seems too easy," you say. "Something as vital as eternal salvation seems far more valuable than that." Don't misunderstand. It is valuable . . . the most priceless possession one can have. But because we don't have to work for it or pay for it does not mean it's cheap or that nobody paid a handsome price. Someone did. His name? Jesus. Perhaps you already forgot that this gift of salvation is directly connected to God's Son,

Christ Himself. Because He paid the full price, because He opened the way for us, we are able to take it as a gift.

It's funny, but most of us are suspicious of free gifts. "Ain't no such thing as a free lunch" is more than a line out of a comedian's script. We have too much skepticism (or pride) to believe we can get something for nothing. Any time we are approached by an individual who promises, "Here, take it; it's yours, free," we are wary. We usually don't reach out and accept it. So it's understandable that we'd be reluctant to accept a gift as important as eternal salvation if it has the appearance of a "free lunch," right?

The Cost of Eternal Salvation

In all honesty, to say that God's rescue offer costs nobody anything is misleading. It costs us nothing today, but it cost His Son's life. That's the part we forget about.

When sin first reared its ugly head on earth, the holy God of heaven could no longer enjoy a close relationship with the human race. And the longer each person practiced his or her sinfulness, the wider the gap grew between humankind and God. This sin disease, contracted at birth and inescapably contagious, spread like wildfire from one generation to the next. With sin came death, as the following statement from Scripture declares:

> When Adam sinned, sin entered the entire human race. Adam's sin brought death, so death spread to everyone, for everyone sinned. (Romans 5:12 NLT)

Yes, *everyone.* In fact, this universal sin disease impacted every part of our being. Hard as it may be to read these words, please do so:

> As the Scriptures say, "No one is good—not even one. No one has real understanding; no one is seeking God. All have turned away from God; all have gone wrong. No one does good, not even one."

> "Their talk is foul, like the stench from an open grave. Their speech is filled with lies."

> "The poison of a deadly snake drips from their lips."

> "Their mouths are full of cursing and bitterness."

"They are quick to commit murder. Wherever they go, destruction and misery follow them. They do not know what true peace is."

"They have no fear of God to restrain them." (Romans 3:10–18 NLT)

Talk about descriptive! But that's the way we are in God's sight. Think of it this way: We're spiritually lost. Being lost, we are in such a confused spiritual condition that we have no hope of finding our way to Him on our own. Sin separates us from our Creator. His rightful requirement is that sin must be punished. Someone who is qualified must rescue mankind by satisfying God's wrath against sin. Someone must pay the awful price, dying as our substitute, taking our place while bearing our sin before God.

This is precisely what Jesus Christ did.

Don't simply believe my words . . . believe what is written in the Bible:

God made the one who did not know sin to be sin for us, so that in him we would become the righteousness of God. (2 Corinthians 5:21 NET)

The law of Moses could not save us, because of our sinful nature. But

God put into effect a different plan to save us. He sent his own Son in a human body like ours, except that ours are sinful. God destroyed sin's control over us by giving his Son as a sacrifice for our sins. (Romans 8:3 NLT)

For this is the way God loved the world: He gave his one and only Son, so that everyone who believes in him will not perish but have eternal life. . . . The one who believes in the Son has eternal life. The one who rejects the Son will not see life, but God's wrath remains on him. (John 3:16, 36 NET)

Christ also suffered once for sins, the just for the unjust, to bring you to God, by being put to death in the flesh but by being made alive in the spirit. (1 Peter 3:18 NET)

By his will we have been made holy through the offering of the body of Jesus Christ once for all. And every priest stands day after day serving and offering the same sacrifices again and again—sacrifices that can never take away sins. But when this priest had offered one sacrifice for sins for all time, he sat down at the right hand of God. (Hebrews 10:10–12 NET)

The Only Unresolved Issue

Yes, it certainly cost somebody something. I repeat, it cost Jesus Christ His life. But because He paid the price in full on our behalf, we are able to accept God's offer free and clear of any cost to us. The payment has been made on our behalf. The ransom has been provided in full.

The only unresolved issue that remains is this: *Will you accept the gift God offers you today?* Now that the remedy for sin has been provided, all that remains is receiving it . . . not having every related question answered.

Picture a person helplessly trapped on the sixth floor of a burning hotel. The elevators no longer function, the stairways are flaming infernos. To live, the person must leap into a net which firemen down below are holding ready. Imagine the trapped man screaming from his broken window, "I will not jump until you give me a satisfactory explanation of several things: (1) How did this fire get started? (2) Why has it spread so quickly? (3) What happened to the sprinkler system? and (4) How do I know for sure that net will hold me? Until you guys can come up with some pretty substantial answers, I'm staying right here in Room 612!"

In like manner, the question as to why God allowed sin to enter the world or the need for airtight convincing proof is comparatively unimportant, even irrelevant, as we find ourselves lost, moving rapidly toward the grave, and destined for eternal condemnation. Slice it up and analyze it any way you wish, when we reduce our response to God's offer of salvation, it comes down to faith: being willing to abandon oneself, without reservation, to the eternal net God has spread . . . leaping while believing with absolute confidence that He will do as He promised. Remember, the other options are reduced to zero, according to God's plan.

What about Life after Death?

A booklet on this vital subject would be incomplete if nothing was said about life beyond the grave. Numerous books — Christian and non-Christian — are now available, ranging from the bizarre to the skeptical. For the sake of space and dependability, let's limit our thoughts to the biblical record.

Jesus spoke openly about both heaven and hell. So did several others in Scripture. It is clear to all who read the Bible that everyone has an eternal soul . . . in that sense, everyone has eternal life. The real question is, where will you spend your life, eternally? Read the following verses carefully:

> And inasmuch as it is appointed for men to die once and after this comes judgment. (Hebrews 9:27)

> But I tell you that every careless word that people speak, they shall give an accounting for it in the day of judgment. (Matthew 12:36)

> These will go away into eternal punishment, but the righteous into eternal life. (Matthew 25:46)

> But you, why do you judge your brother? Or you again, why do you regard your brother with contempt? For we will all stand before the judgment seat of God. (Romans 14:10)

> Jesus said to her, "I am the resurrection and the life; he who believes in Me will live even if he dies, and everyone who lives and believes in Me will never die. Do you believe this?" (John 11:25–26)

The Reality of Hell

A particular story Jesus once told comes to my mind every time I think of life after death. Because it is descriptive and brief, we are able to get a fairly uncomplicated picture in our minds of this subject.

> Now there was a rich man, and he habitually dressed in purple and fine linen, joyously living in splendor every day. And a poor man named Lazarus was laid at his gate, covered with sores, and longing to be fed with the crumbs which were falling from the rich man's table; besides, even the dogs were coming and licking his sores. Now the poor man died and was carried away by the angels to Abraham's bosom; and the rich man also died and was buried. In Hades he lifted up his eyes, being in torment, and saw Abraham far away and Lazarus in his bosom. And he cried out and said, "Father Abraham, have mercy on me, and send Lazarus so that he may dip the tip of his finger in water and cool off my tongue, for I am in agony in this flame."

But Abraham said, "Child, remember that during your life you received your good things, and likewise Lazarus bad things; but now he is being comforted here, and you are in agony. And besides all this, between us and you there is a great chasm fixed, so that those who wish to come over from here to you will not be able, and that none may cross over from there to us."

And he said, "Then I beg you, father, that you send him to my father's house — for I have five brothers — in order that he may warn them, so that they will not also come to this place of torment."

But Abraham said, "They have Moses and the Prophets; let them hear them."

But he said, "No, father Abraham, but if someone goes to them from the dead, they will repent!"

But he said to him, "If they do not listen to Moses and the Prophets, they will not be persuaded even if someone rises from the dead." (Luke 16:19–31)

Much of what you just read needs no explanation. It is the story of two men. While alive, their status could hardly have been more different. And when they died, again a major contrast. One found himself in heaven; the other, in hell. Our attention falls upon the rich man who is pleading for relief and removal from his torturous surroundings. The scene is unpleasant to imagine, but it is nevertheless real. Neither here nor elsewhere does Jesus suggest this was merely a fantasy.

The man in hell is in conscious torment. He is crying out for mercy. Being "far away" (16:23) and permanently removed by "a great chasm" (16:26), he is desperately alone, unable to escape from hell, as we read, "none may cross over" (16:26). The horror is painfully literal, unlike the jokes often passed around regarding hell. Haunted with thoughts of other family members ultimately coming to the same place, the man begs for someone to go to his father's house and warn his brothers "so that they will not also come to this place of torment" (16:28).

This is only one of many references to an eternal existence in hell. The New Testament, in fact, says more about hell than it does about heaven. Here are just a few characteristics of hell set forth in the New Testament:

- It is a place of weeping and gnashing of teeth (Matthew 8:12).

- It is a place where people scream for mercy, have memories, are tormented, feel alone, and cannot escape (Luke 16:23–31).

- It is a place of eternal, unquenchable fire (Mark 9:48).

- It is a place of darkness (Revelation 9:2).

- It is a place where God's wrath is poured out (Revelation 14:10).

- It is a place of everlasting destruction (2 Thessalonians 1:9).

The finality of all this is overwhelmingly depressing. We have little struggle believing that heaven will be forever, but for some reason, many ignore that hell will be equally everlasting. To deny the permanence of hell is impossible without also removing the permanence of heaven. Each is a reality, and each is ultimate finality.

Some views try to explain away or bypass hell. One attempt is *annihilation*. This says that the righteous will live eternally, but the wicked will ultimately be judged and destroyed. Nice idea but a theological cop-out. It cannot be maintained by a serious and intelligent study of Scripture . . .

for example, the whole issue of a bodily resurrection. What purpose is the resurrection if the lost are to be extinguished forever?

Another attempt at bypassing hell is *universalism*, which teaches that all humanity will ultimately be saved. This position offers a comforting "redemptive mercy" that will eventually include all mankind. If this were true, what did Jesus mean when He talked about the very real possibility of being lost forever? "Should not perish" in John 3:16 implies that some will indeed perish. And how could His comment be taken seriously when He says to the unsaved, "Depart from Me, accursed ones, into the *eternal* fire" (Matthew 25:41, emphasis added)? Count on it, eternal means eternal.

The Reality of Heaven

The same Bible that addresses the subject of hell also reveals the truth about heaven. What is heaven like? Playing harps all day? Lounging around on puffy clouds? Living in enormous mansions along solid gold streets? Does it mean we'll all have long white robes with matching sandals, glowing halos, and big flapping wings? Hardly!

Heaven is an actual place. A prepared place, designed for God's redeemed people, those who have accepted God's free gift of His Son. As Jesus told His faithful followers,

> Do not let your heart be troubled; believe in God, believe also in Me. In My Father's house are many dwelling places; if it were not so, I would have told you; for I go to prepare a place for you. If I go and prepare a place for you, I will come again and receive you to Myself, that where I am, there you may be also. (John 14:1–3)

According to this and other reliable New Testament statements, heaven will be a place of beauty, peace, perfect health, and endless happiness, filled with people from all the earthly ages who have one thing in common: faith in the Lord Jesus Christ, the Lamb of God, who took away the sin of the world.

Think of it! Characters from the Old Testament like Moses, David, Rahab, Elijah, Abraham, Joseph, Esther, Job, Daniel, and the other godly prophets will converse with John, Peter, Matthew, James, Paul, Silas, Barnabas, Mary, Elizabeth, Lydia, and Andrew. We'll be able to enjoy close conversations with church history's great

Christians, like Augustine, David Livingstone, Hudson Taylor, Martin Luther, John Calvin, John Knox, Charles Spurgeon, Dwight Moody, John Wycliffe, and John Huss (to name only a few), plus all of the unknown martyrs, missionaries, pastors, authors, statesmen, politicians, poets, and leaders from every generation since time began. What a stupendous thought!

More amazing still, in heaven we'll have a face-to-face, exclusive relationship with our Savior, gloriously enjoyed without interruption or heartache or grief or sin or the threat of death.

> Then I saw a new heaven and a new earth; for the first heaven and the first earth passed away, and there is no longer any sea. And I saw the holy city, new Jerusalem, coming down out of heaven from God, made ready as a bride adorned for her husband. And I heard a loud voice from the throne, saying, "Behold, the tabernacle of God is among men, and He will dwell among them, and they shall be His people, and God Himself will be among them, and He will wipe away every tear from their eyes; and there will no longer

be any death; there will no longer be any mourning, or crying, or pain; the first things have passed away."

And He who sits on the throne said, "Behold, I am making all things new." And He said, "Write, for these words are faithful and true." Then He said to me, "It is done. I am the Alpha and the Omega, the beginning and the end. I will give to the one who thirsts from the spring of the water of life without cost." (Revelation 21:1–6)

There it is again. "Without cost." Heaven will be the destiny of those who take God at His Word, believing in His Son, Jesus Christ, and coming in faith, by grace, to salvation . . . without cost.

Can something this good really be free? Even free of works? Great question. You decide after reading these Scripture verses.

For by grace you have been saved through faith; and that not of yourselves, it is the gift of God; not as a result of works, so that no one may boast. (Ephesians 2:8–9)

Now to the one who works, his wage is not credited as a favor, but as what is due. But to the one who does not work, but believes in Him who justifies the ungodly, his faith is credited as righteousness. (Romans 4:4–5)

He saved us, not on the basis of deeds which we have done in righteousness, but according to His mercy, by the washing of regeneration and renewing by the Holy Spirit, whom He poured out upon us richly through Jesus Christ our Savior, so that being justified by His grace we would be made heirs according to the hope of eternal life. (Titus 3:5–7)

Knowing that you were not redeemed with perishable things like silver or gold from your futile way of life inherited from your forefathers, but with precious blood, as of a lamb unblemished and spotless, the blood of Christ. (1 Peter 1:18–19)

Nevertheless knowing that a man is not justified by the works of the Law but through faith in Christ Jesus, even we have believed in Christ Jesus, so that we may be justified by faith in Christ and not by the works of the Law; since by the works of the Law no flesh will be justified. (Galatians 2:16)

[God] has saved us and called us with a holy calling, not according to our works, but according to His own purpose and grace which was granted us in Christ Jesus from all eternity, but now has been revealed by the appearing of our Savior Christ Jesus, who abolished death and brought life and immortality to light through the gospel. (2 Timothy 1:9–10)

Yes, salvation comes to us "free and clear" of any hidden charges or religious deeds or human effort. We come to God through Christ . . . lost, sinful, without hope, and deserving of hell. Grace makes all that possible. God sees us in Christ and in grace loves us, forgives us, accepts us into His family, and promises us an eternal home with Him in heaven, the ultimate destination of all His people.

Your Final Destination: Where?

Salvation is the single most important issue in all of life. Yet, if you are not careful, you will put it off until later; you'll even put it completely out of your mind. Salvation is an urgent matter. We dare not postpone our decision!

In review:

- You are lost.

- You are sinful.

- You need help.

- God is holy.

- Christ has died for your sins.

- Christ rose again.

- Salvation is free to you.

- Hell is horrible.

- Heaven is available.

- You must believe.

  For I delivered to you as of first importance what I also received, that Christ died for our sins according to the Scriptures, and that He was buried, and that He was raised on the third day according to the Scriptures. (1 Corinthians 15:3–4)

God has given us eternal life, and this life is in His Son. He who has the Son has the life; he who does not have the Son of God does not have the life. These things I have written to you who believe in the name of the Son of God, so that you may know that you have eternal life. (1 John 5:11–13)

You can know.

Will you believe?

That is a penetrating question. As you ponder it, consider this: your future will be the product of your perspective today. The following story illustrates this truth.

The reality of life beyond the grave should make every one of us ponder our eternal destination, because the Bible teaches only two possibilities, heaven and hell.

We take care to provide for the relatively short span of retirement after 65. How foolish not to plan for the endless ages of eternity. Confrontation with what comes after death caused one young man to prepare for the hereafter by receiving Jesus Christ as his Savior. He was looking at a large estate one day and said to a friend, "Oh, if I were lucky enough to call this estate mine, I should be a happy fellow. It's worth a quarter million."

"And then?" said his friend.

"Why, then I'd pull down the old house and build a mansion, have lots of friends around me, get married, have several fine cars and keep the finest horses and dogs in the country."

"And then?"

"Then I would hunt, and ride, and fish, and keep open house, and enjoy life gloriously."

"And then?"

"Why, then, I suppose like other people, I should grow old and not care so much for these things."

"And then?"

"Why, in the course of nature I should die."

"And then?"

"Oh, bother your 'and then.' I have no time for you now!"

Years later the friend was surprised to hear from him, "God bless you. I owe my happiness to you."

"How?"

"By two words asked at the right time — 'And then?'" [1]

God's eternal gift of salvation is yours for the taking. I ask you, will you do so today?

⌒

Loving God, thank You for accepting me and forgiving me many years ago when I was lost, and afraid, and confused, and so far away from You. I am thankful that You heard my prayer and took me seriously, even though I did not know how to express my faith in Jesus very well. All I knew to do was to come as a little child, which I did. And You graciously took me in. Thank You for forgiving my sins and making it possible to KNOW You, personally — today.

Now I come to You on behalf of the person who is reading these words right now. Please help him or her come to terms with what has been read. Take away the fear and the doubt. Push aside the tendency to procrastinate. Reveal the urgency of this decision. May Your Son's death and resurrection be convincing so that this person may KNOW eternal life with You — today — and secure his or her destiny forever.

I ask this in the strong name of Jesus Christ, my Lord and Savior.

Amen.

WE ARE HERE
FOR YOU

If you desire to find out more about knowing God and His plan for you in the Bible, contact us. Insight for Living provides staff pastors and women's counselors who are available for free written correspondence or phone consultation. These seminary-trained and seasoned men and women have years of pastoral experience and are well-qualified guides for your spiritual journey.

Please feel welcome to contact our Pastoral Ministries department by calling the Insight for Living Care Line: 972-473-5097, 8 A.M. through 5 P.M. Central Time. Or you may write to the following address:

> Insight for Living
> Pastoral Ministries Department
> Post Office Box 269000
> Plano, Texas 75026-9000

ENDNOTES

1. Leslie B. Flynn, *What Is Man?* (Wheaton, Ill.: Victor Books, 1978), 100–101.